NUCLEAR WASTE DISPOSAL

© Aladdin Books Ltd 1990

Designed and produced by
Aladdin Books Ltd
28 Percy Street
London W1P 9FF

First published in
Great Britain in 1990 by
Franklin Watts Ltd
96 Leonard Street
London EC2A 4RH

ISBN 0 7496 0442 5

A CIP catalogue record for this
book is available from the British
Library.

Printed in Belgium

The publishers would like to
acknowledge that the
photographs reproduced within
this book have been posed by
models or have been obtained
from photographic agencies.

Design	David West Children's Book Design
Editor	Elise Bradbury
Picture research	Emma Krikler
Illustrator	Ian Moores

The author, Dr Tony Hare, is a
writer, ecologist and TV
presenter. He works with several
environmental organisations
including the London Wildlife
Trust, the British Association of
Nature Conservationists, and
Plantlife, of which he is Chairman
of the Board.

The consultants: Jacky Karas is a
Senior Research Associate at the
School of Environmental Sciences
at the University of East Anglia.

Rachel Western is a consultant to
the Friends of the Earth Energy
Campaign.

SAVE OUR EARTH

NUCLEAR WASTE DISPOSAL

TONY HARE

GLOUCESTER PRESS

London · New York · Toronto · Sydney

CONTENTS

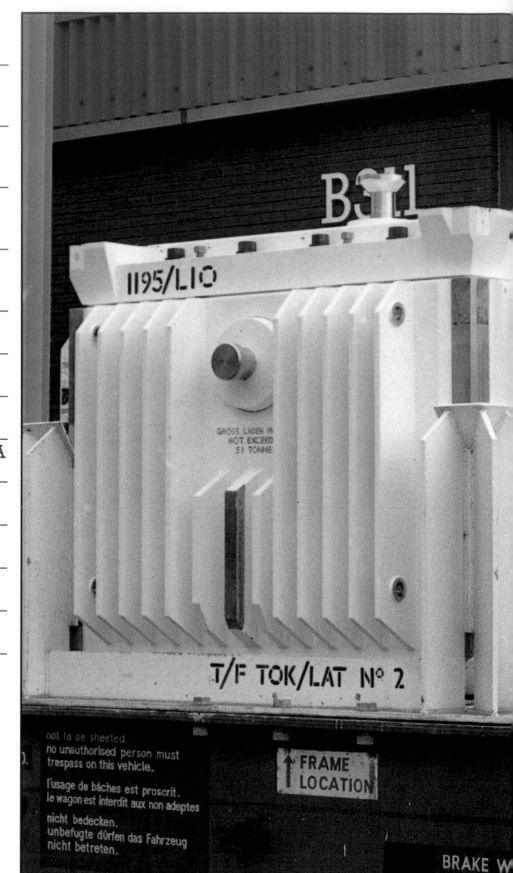

INTRODUCTION

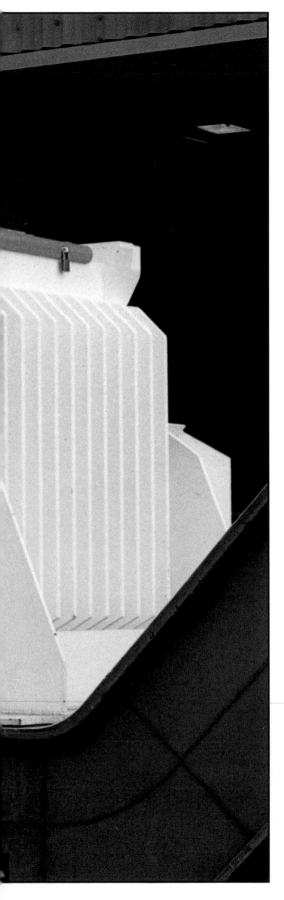

When scientists developed the first nuclear bomb in the 1940s, we moved into what has been called the nuclear age. Nuclear energy is the energy released by the incredibly powerful forces that hold atoms together. Since scientists discovered how to harness the power of nuclear reactions for bombs, this energy has also been used to produce electricity in nuclear power stations.

Nuclear energy has been praised as clean power because its generation does not release polluting gases that are produced when fossil fuels (coal, oil and gas) are burned. However, during nuclear reactions a type of pollution, called radioactivity, is produced. Radioactivity can be dangerous; some kinds damage living things. Also, radioactive substances can remain harmful for thousands of years, and can contaminate other materials they come into contact with.

Nuclear power stations produce waste, just as other power stations do. Some types of nuclear waste are extremely radioactive, and living things and the environment have to be protected from this radioactivity. The nuclear waste that is produced now needs to be stored safely to keep future generations from coming into contact with it.

◄ **This container holds highly radioactive material. We are exposed to small amounts of radioactivity naturally. It is given off by rocks, the air and cosmic rays (from the Sun and space). However, nuclear waste adds to this radioactivity.**

5

USING NUCLEAR ENERGY

Everything is made up of atoms, which are incredibly tiny – 100,000 million of them would fit in a full-stop. Atoms themselves are made up of even tinier particles; electrons, protons and neutrons, and these particles are held together by extremely powerful forces. When atoms are broken apart, an enormous amount of heat energy is produced. Nuclear reactors harness this energy to produce electricity.

Scientists can only split the atoms in certain substances. Uranium (a naturally radioactive metal) is the fuel most often used in nuclear reactors because in nature, uranium atoms are so big that they are unstable and break up very slowly. This produces small amounts of energy and radiation. But in nuclear reactors they are split quickly, producing much more energy. This is called nuclear fission.

▼ **In nuclear fission in a reactor, atoms are bombarded with neutrons. When an atom is hit by a neutron it becomes very unstable. It splits apart, releasing a great deal of energy and more neutrons, which can then go on to split more atoms.**

Uranium is mined in many countries (below right) and made into fuel pellets (below left), which are put in fuel rods for use in nuclear reactors.

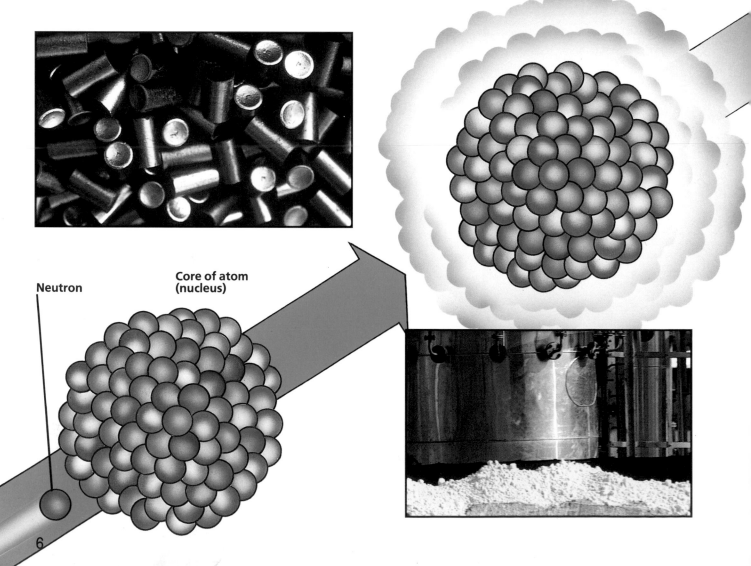

Nucleus made unstable

Neutron

Core of atom (nucleus)

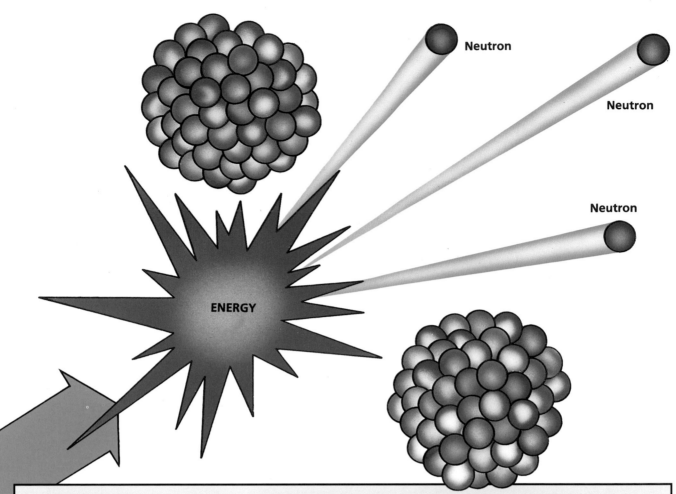

Neutron

Neutron

Neutron

ENERGY

The fission process takes place inside the nuclear reactor core (right). It has to be carried out very carefully. If the reactions were uncontrolled the uranium atoms would break down one after the other so quickly that a huge amount of energy would be released all at once, leading to an explosion. To prevent this, the fuel rods in most reactors are surrounded by moderators and control rods which slow down or capture the escaping neutrons so that the atoms break down at a safe rate. The heat released from the splitting atoms is taken from the reactor, often by water or gas, and used to make steam, which turns turbines to make electricity.

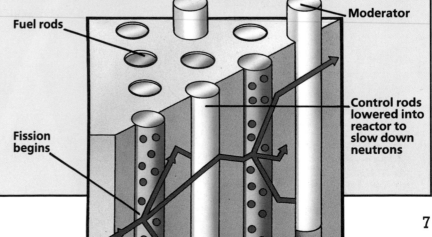

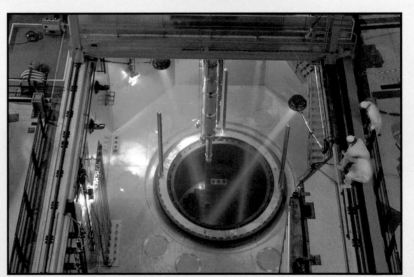

Fuel rods

Moderator

Control rods lowered into reactor to slow down neutrons

Fission begins

7

WHAT IS NUCLEAR WASTE?

Waste is produced by many activities. Factories and power stations produce waste, some of it dangerous, which is released into the environment. Nuclear power stations create nuclear waste, which is radioactive. It is dangerous and can remain so for a very long time.

Nuclear waste comes in many different forms. When the uranium fuel rods are used up, or spent, they contain the most dangerous radioactive waste, known as high-level waste. When a nuclear power station reaches the end of its useful life it is closed down, known as decommissioning. The reactor core is so radioactive it cannot be taken apart.

Other things in a nuclear power station also get contaminated by radioactivity. For example, the workers who handle radioactive material have to replace their clothes regularly, and those that are thrown away become waste. These types of waste are less radioactive than high-level waste and are called intermediate- or low-level waste depending on how radioactive they are.

▼ **Nuclear power stations are not the only producers of radioactive waste. Uranium mining leaves radioactive tailings (finely ground rock) which can contaminate the surrounding area. When nuclear weapons are taken apart the pieces are radioactive. Some types of medical waste, like cotton swabs and hospital gloves, have been made radioactive by chemicals used in certain types of medical treatment.**

Spent fuel rods

Uranium mine

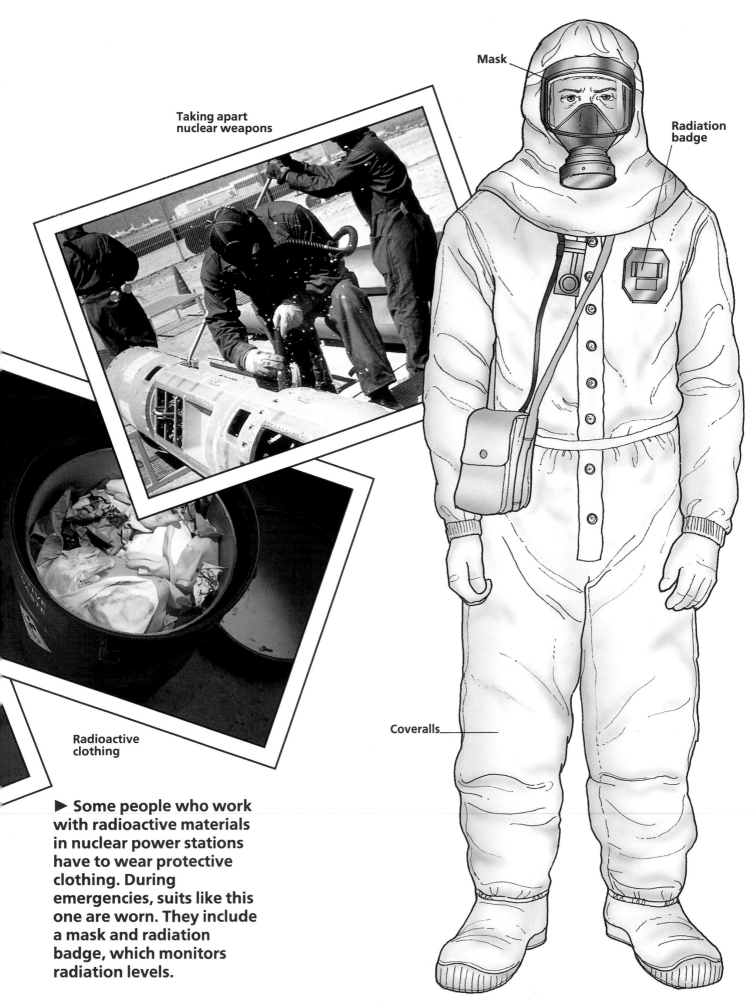

Mask

Radiation
badge

Taking apart
nuclear weapons

Radioactive
clothing

Coveralls

▶ Some people who work
with radioactive materials
in nuclear power stations
have to wear protective
clothing. During
emergencies, suits like this
one are worn. They include
a mask and radiation
badge, which monitors
radiation levels.

WHAT IS RADIOACTIVITY?

Radioactivity is a form of radiation (energy that is transmitted through rays). Some substances are naturally radioactive, and a few are made radioactive after being bombarded with tiny particles. One of these substances is plutonium, which is an extremely radioactive element used in making nuclear bombs.

Radioactivity is released every time a radioactive substance decays. As it decays it changes form by releasing a burst of energy and shooting out tiny particles. If the substance is still radioactive it decays again, releasing more radioactivity. After a series of decays it is no longer radioactive; it stops decaying and is said to be stable.

▶ **Radium is a naturally radioactive substance which was used in the past to make glow-in-the-dark watch dials. Like all radioactive substances, radium gradually decays and loses its radioactivity. After a period of time (1,600 years) half the atoms in a lump of radium will have decayed. Then, after the same amount of time has passed again, half of those that are left will have decayed. This carries on, lessening the amount of radioactivity left, shown by the green arrows (right). The time it takes for half the radioactive atoms to decay is known as the half-life. Each radioactive substance has a different half-life. One type of uranium has a half-life of 4,470,000,000 years. At the other end of the scale, caesium 142 has a half-life of only one minute.**

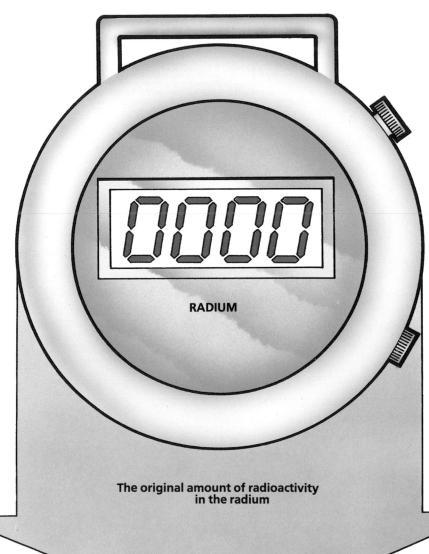

RADIUM

The original amount of radioactivity in the radium

▲ Rocks like granite contain small amounts of radioactivity.

3200

RADIUM

After two half-lives,
one quarter of the atoms
remain undecayed

1600

RADIUM

1,600 years later
half-life is reached –
half of the atoms
remain undecayed

▼ Radioactivity cannot be seen, smelled or felt. But a machine called a Geiger counter allows us to measure it. The counter gives a click every time it detects atoms decaying.

TYPES OF RADIOACTIVITY

Radiation consists of tiny particles and rays given off by the decaying atoms in a radioactive substance. There are three types: alpha particles, beta particles and gamma rays, named after the first three letters in the Greek alphabet. Alpha and beta particles are parts of atoms which have split off in a nuclear reaction. Gamma rays are waves, rather like light or X-rays, and they travel at the speed of light. Some radioactive substances produce only one or two types of radiation. Nuclear waste usually contains a variety of different radioactive materials, so it produces large amounts of all three types of radiation, alpha, beta and gamma, each of which can be damaging in different ways.

Radioactivity cannot be destroyed by ordinary means. We cannot get rid of it by burning radioactive waste or treating it with chemicals, like we do with other types of waste. It disappears of its own accord as radioactive atoms decay, which can take thousands of years. This is why nuclear waste presents a long-term problem.

▼ **Radiation can destroy cancer cells. This form of cancer treatment is called radiotherapy and is employed in many hospitals (below). Another benefit of radioactivity in medicine is the use of radiotracers. A small amount of a radioactive substance, like radio-iodine, is put into the body where it concentrates in certain organs. Machines can detect the radiation and check if the organ is working properly.**

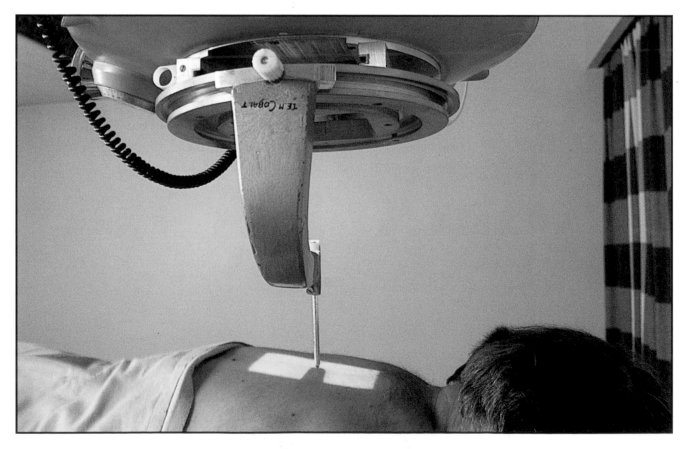

The different types of radioactivity have varying powers of penetration. Alpha particles are stopped by a sheet of paper or by skin. A few metres of air or a thin sheet of glass or metal stops beta particles. Gamma rays penetrate the furthest. They can travel a long way and a shield of lead or concrete is necessary to stop them. When working with substances that produce gamma rays, workers stay behind glass and use remote control to handle the material (above).

■ ALPHA
■ BETA
□ GAMMA

13

EFFECTS OF RADIOACTIVITY

Although radioactivity is useful in medicine, it can also have very harmful effects on living things. If a person is exposed to a high level of radiation they may suffer radiation sickness. Symptoms include vomiting, loss of hair, bleeding and death. This is what happened to workers who died trying to contain the nuclear accident at the Chernobyl reactor in the USSR, and to thousands in Hiroshima and Nagasaki in Japan who died soon after the first atom bombs were dropped in 1945.

Lower doses of radiation can cause cancer, including leukaemia (a cancer of the blood cells) in children. If the reproductive organs are exposed to radiation, it may cause damage which can be passed on to the children of the person affected.

People can come into contact with radioactivity through food, drink, air or water that has been contaminated, as well as from natural sources. Under normal conditions nuclear power stations release a very small amount of radioactivity into the environment.

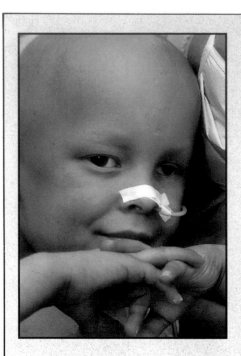

▶ **If radiation penetrates the skin or is inhaled or swallowed, it can cause a great deal of damage. The main problem is that radiation causes massive disruption in the cells of the body. This can lead to cancer if the damaged cells reproduce. Gamma rays can penetrate the skin very easily and damage cell after cell as they move through the body. Beta particles can cause skin burns and, if they get into the body, cell damage. Alpha particles cannot penetrate the skin, but they can cause severe internal damage if swallowed or breathed in.**

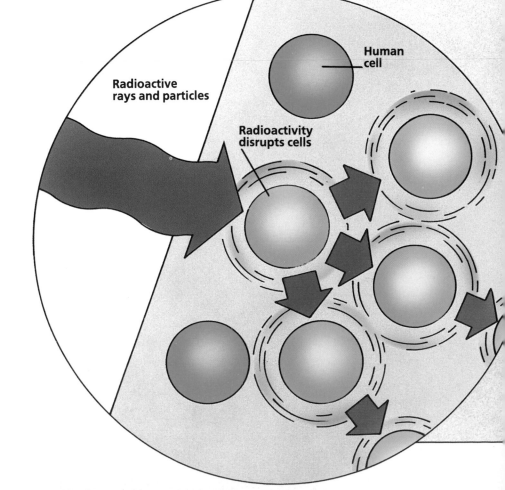

Radioactive rays and particles

Human cell

Radioactivity disrupts cells

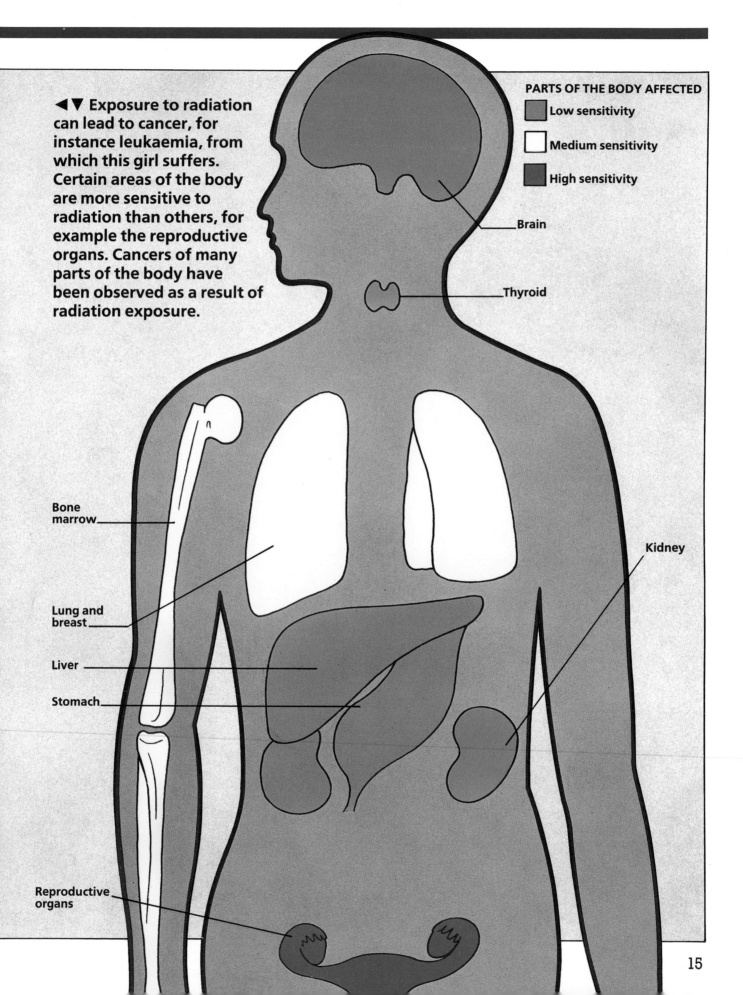

Exposure to radiation can lead to cancer, for instance leukaemia, from which this girl suffers. Certain areas of the body are more sensitive to radiation than others, for example the reproductive organs. Cancers of many parts of the body have been observed as a result of radiation exposure.

PARTS OF THE BODY AFFECTED

Low sensitivity

Medium sensitivity

High sensitivity

Brain

Thyroid

Bone marrow

Lung and breast

Liver

Stomach

Kidney

Reproductive organs

HIGH-LEVEL WASTE

◄ **Water storage of spent fuel rods at Sellafield. After treatment, low-level radioactivity from the cooling water is discharged directly into the sea.**

The uranium fuel rods that produce the energy in a nuclear power station eventually come to the end of their useful lives. They contain the most highly radioactive waste, the split uranium atoms, and are so radioactive that they generate their own heat. These rods are placed in huge pools of water where they gradually cool down and become less radioactive.

Some countries treat the whole of the fuel rods as waste and store them on site. Other countries, including France, process them to extract the unused fuel. This is called reprocessing. It involves dissolving the spent rods in acid and recovering the uranium and plutonium. The acid, with the radioactive waste in it, can then be stored in tanks or turned into a type of glass.

High-level waste, whether it is in the form of entire fuel rods, glass or acid solution, will remain dangerously radioactive for tens of thousands of years.

► **Reprocessing is seen by some people as useful because the nuclear fuel extracted from the old fuel rods may be used to make new ones. However, a major drawback is that reprocessing plants produce huge quantities of low- and intermediate-level waste which would not be generated if the spent fuel rods were simply stored. The plants also release large amounts of radioactivity into the air and sea. Discharge from Sellafield, the British reprocessing centre that accepts nuclear waste from many other countries, has made the Irish Sea the most radioactively contaminated sea in the world.**

THE GLOBAL DUMP

Low- and intermediate-level radioactive waste, from nuclear power and medical and research use, are not as dangerous as high-level waste in the short term, but they still present a health threat. In the early years of nuclear power, low- and intermediate-level wastes were dumped in the ground or in the sea. But public pressure and increasing knowledge of the dangers radioactive wastes pose has led the nuclear industry to realise that they must be disposed of more carefully or stored while research is continued.

The usual way of disposing of such wastes is by burial. The lowest-level wastes, such as radioactive tissues and test-tubes, are buried in metal containers in shallow trenches. Other waste is planned for deeper burial, and different countries have different locations; sites that are being used or considered include old salt and iron mines, holes drilled in hillsides, and specially-built deep underground storage sites.

▼ **Some countries have built concrete storage sites for low- and intermediate-level nuclear waste. Britain's low-level waste is taken to Drigg (below), near Sellafield in Cumbria. Drigg accepts waste from hospitals and industries as well as from the nuclear industry.**

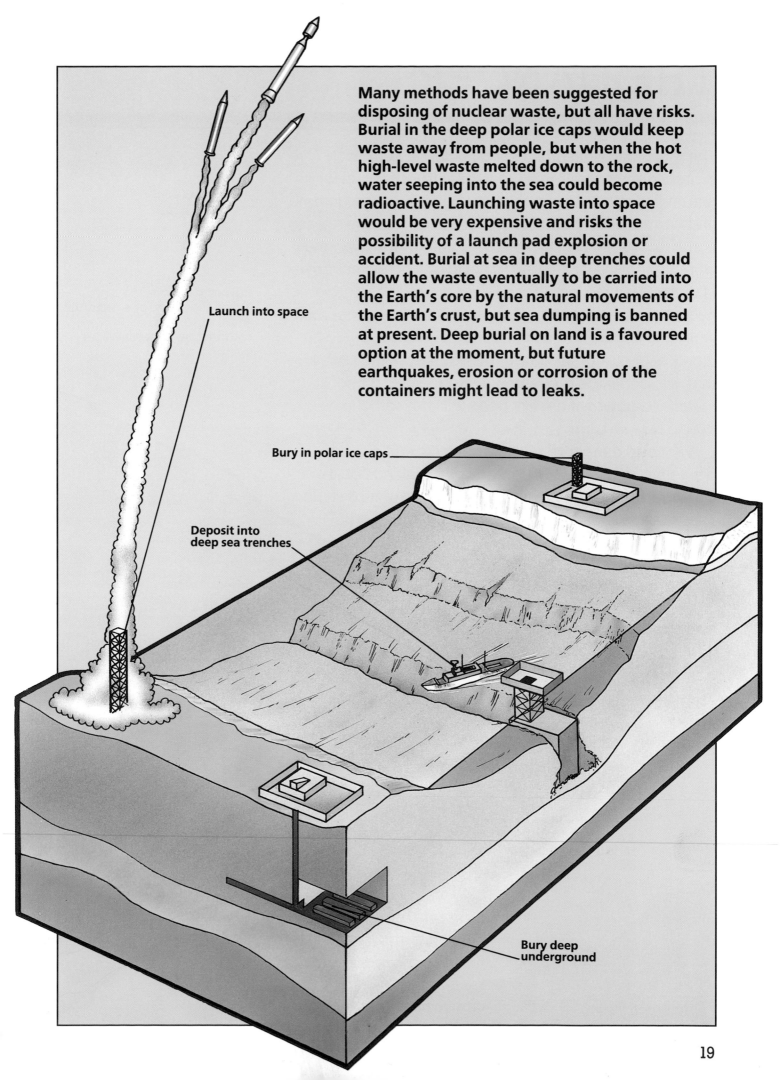

Many methods have been suggested for disposing of nuclear waste, but all have risks. Burial in the deep polar ice caps would keep waste away from people, but when the hot high-level waste melted down to the rock, water seeping into the sea could become radioactive. Launching waste into space would be very expensive and risks the possibility of a launch pad explosion or accident. Burial at sea in deep trenches could allow the waste eventually to be carried into the Earth's core by the natural movements of the Earth's crust, but sea dumping is banned at present. Deep burial on land is a favoured option at the moment, but future earthquakes, erosion or corrosion of the containers might lead to leaks.

Launch into space

Bury in polar ice caps

Deposit into deep sea trenches

Bury deep underground

THE DANGERS

The main concern surrounding nuclear energy is to protect people and the environment from contact with harmful amounts of radioactivity. Nuclear waste dumps and normal operations at nuclear power stations release some radioactivity into the environment. However, the worst fear is the possibility of accidents at nuclear power stations, in nuclear submarines or during the transport of nuclear waste cargoes, which are especially dangerous when they consist of spent fuel rods on their way to be reprocessed. A great deal of money is spent to ensure that accidents are prevented. Unfortunately these measures have not always been failsafe, sometimes due to human error.

A second danger of nuclear power is that nuclear waste has a lifetime of hundreds or thousands of years. So far, the methods proposed to dispose of this waste cannot be guaranteed safe this far into the future.

Power stations
Normal operations produce small amounts of radioactive air and water pollution.

Nuclear submarines
Accidents may damage the nuclear reactor which runs the submarine, or the nuclear weapons it carries, leading to contamination of the sea.

Sea dumping
Canisters dumped at sea (before the international ban came into effect) may lead to dangerous contamination.

Deep burial underground storage
Earthquakes, erosion, flooding, mining or corrosion of the containers could cause leakage and contamination.

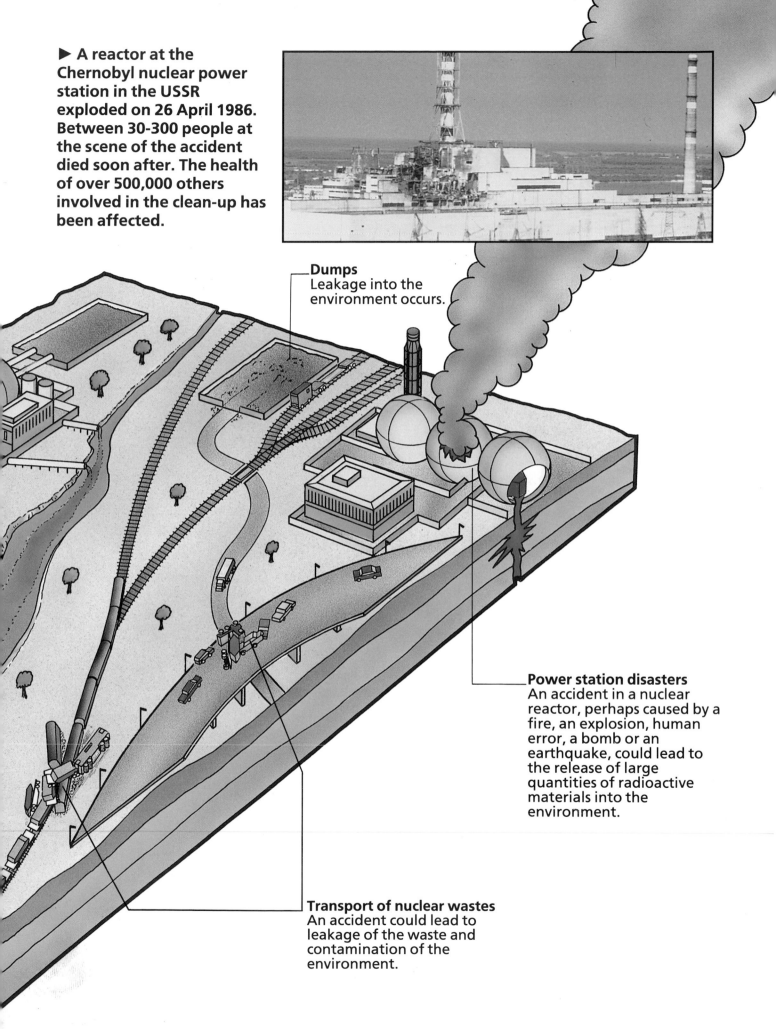

► A reactor at the Chernobyl nuclear power station in the USSR exploded on 26 April 1986. Between 30-300 people at the scene of the accident died soon after. The health of over 500,000 others involved in the clean-up has been affected.

Dumps
Leakage into the environment occurs.

Power station disasters
An accident in a nuclear reactor, perhaps caused by a fire, an explosion, human error, a bomb or an earthquake, could lead to the release of large quantities of radioactive materials into the environment.

Transport of nuclear wastes
An accident could lead to leakage of the waste and contamination of the environment.

21

THE ENERGY DILEMMA

All of the main methods of producing energy cause hazards. Mining and transporting fossil fuels can lead to accidents, including tanker accidents, which can cause oil pollution. Burning fossil fuels produces air pollution, leading to the formation of acid rain. This can damage trees and buildings and is a health hazard. Burning fossil fuels also produces carbon dioxide which traps heat in the atmosphere, possibly leading to an increase in the world temperature – this is known as global warming. Scientists fear this may cause flooding, weather changes and other catastrophes.

These facts, in addition to the limited amount of fossil fuel reserves, cause some people to think that nuclear power, with its relatively low amount of immediate pollution, is the ideal option for electricity generation. However, we have to weigh against this its risks.

Fossil fuel power stations produce carbon dioxide which traps heat in the atmosphere, possibly leading to global warming.

▼ Mining fuel for power stations has many risks. People who work in mines, whether for coal or uranium, sometimes suffer from lung diseases caused by the dust and gas they breathe in while working. Also, accidents like roof collapses can kill miners.

Extraction of oil leads to waste and the possibility of accidents which endanger lives and pollute the environment.

Transportation of oil can lead to pollution disasters such as oil spills which affect both wildlife and people.

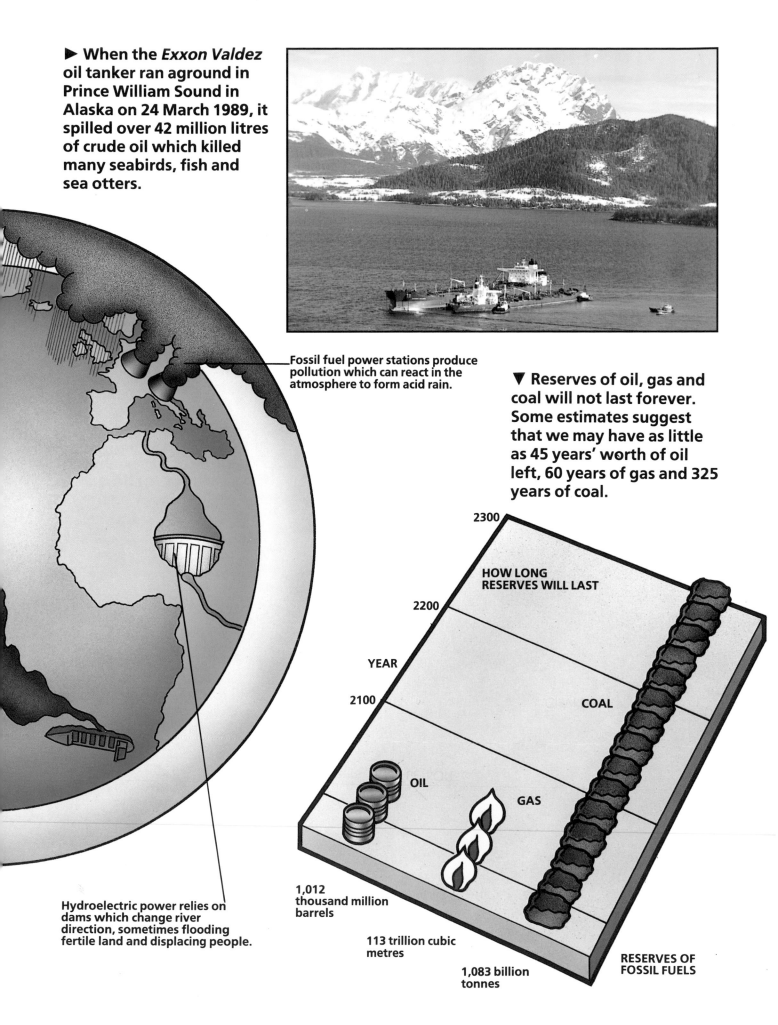

▶ When the *Exxon Valdez* oil tanker ran aground in Prince William Sound in Alaska on 24 March 1989, it spilled over 42 million litres of crude oil which killed many seabirds, fish and sea otters.

Fossil fuel power stations produce pollution which can react in the atmosphere to form acid rain.

▼ Reserves of oil, gas and coal will not last forever. Some estimates suggest that we may have as little as 45 years' worth of oil left, 60 years of gas and 325 years of coal.

HOW LONG RESERVES WILL LAST

2300

2200

YEAR

2100

COAL

OIL

GAS

1,012 thousand million barrels

113 trillion cubic metres

1,083 billion tonnes

RESERVES OF FOSSIL FUELS

Hydroelectric power relies on dams which change river direction, sometimes flooding fertile land and displacing people.

23

ALTERNATIVES

Nuclear power is often put forward as a solution to the energy problems we face. However, managing nuclear waste needs to be made an urgent priority. Many believe that the safest solution is to store the waste on site so that leaks can be discovered and stopped.

Alternative energy sources do not have the same drawbacks as the types of energy production we rely on now. There is an unlimited amount of natural energy on the planet: the energy of the Sun, the tides, the wind and of the heat inside the Earth (geothermal energy).

Like hydroelectric power, these alternatives do present some problems themselves. Schemes to harness tidal power, for example, could easily disrupt the coastal environment. What is needed is further development of alternative energy sources together with real efforts to clean up the sources we use at present.

A vital factor is energy efficiency. If we use energy more carefully we can reduce the amount we consume, and that would cut down the need for power stations and the problems that go with them.

▼ **Many scientists hope the next step for nuclear energy is fusion power. This involves making two atoms join together, or fuse, rather than splitting one apart. Deuterium and tritium are two elements which have been used in fusion experiments. The photograph (below right) shows the huge amount of energy released from nuclear fusion during laser experiments. But no one has yet found out how to make fusion work on a large scale. The latest estimates predict it will be at least 70 years before fusion power is a reality.**

NUCLEAR FUSION

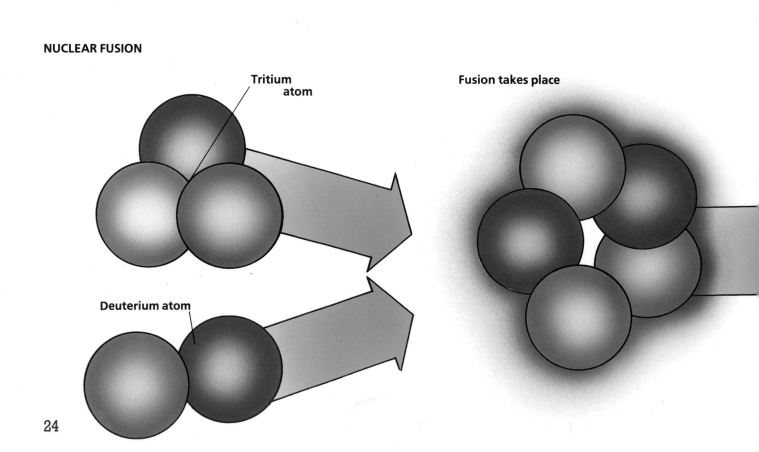

Tritium atom

Fusion takes place

Deuterium atom

Recently, oil provided 35 per cent of the world's energy needs, natural gas 17 per cent, coal 27 per cent, and nuclear power three per cent. Renewable sources of energy (sources which will not run out) contributed only 18 per cent. Nearly all of this was from hydroelectric power, with wood-burning and waste-burning making up most of the rest. The figures for alternative sources like solar power, wind power and tidal power were tiny. Yet their potential is huge. Some farms on the Falkland Islands, for example, have wind generators. Alternative power could supply much more; it has been estimated that wind power could provide up to one fifth of all Britain's energy needs.

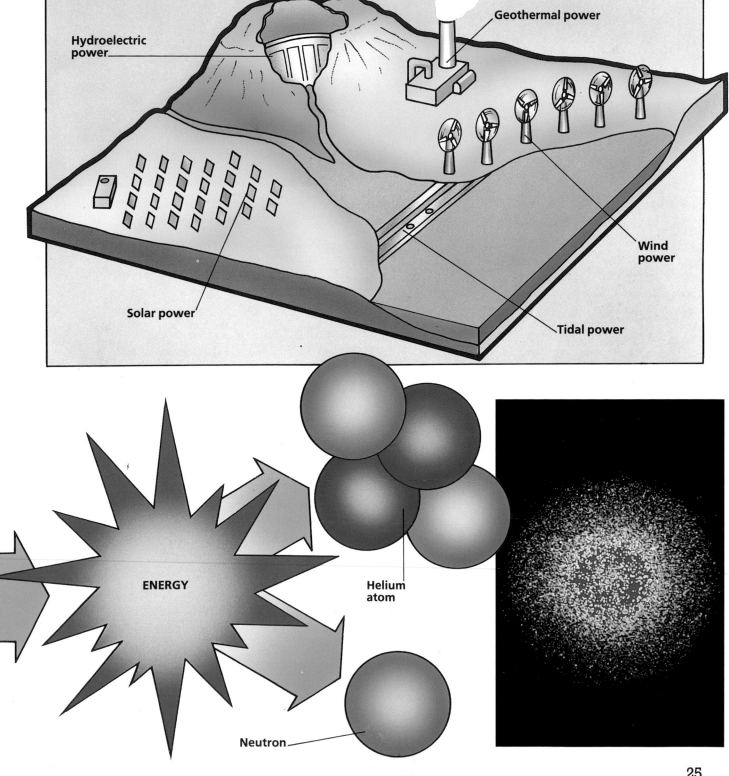

Hydroelectric power

Geothermal power

Wind power

Solar power

Tidal power

ENERGY

Helium atom

Neutron

WHAT YOU CAN DO

You may not think you have much say in the way nuclear waste is managed. However, the nuclear waste that is produced today will still be around when your children are adults, and when their children are adults... so it is worth making your opinion known by writing to your MP or to the organisations below. You can also help to cut down your country's energy consumption by being energy-efficient: start by turning out lights when they are not needed and by getting your parents to insulate the house effectively, which cuts down heating needs.

Useful addresses

Association for the Conservation of Energy
9 Sherlock Mews
London W1M 3RH
Tel: 071-935 1495

British Nuclear Fuels
Risley
Warrington
Cheshire WA3 6AS
Tel: 0925 832000

Friends of the Earth
26-28 Underwood Street
London N1 7JQ
Tel: 071-490 1555

Greenpeace
30-31 Islington Green
London N1 8XE
Tel: 071-354 5100

United Kingdom NIREX*
Curie Avenue
Harwell
Didcot
Oxfordshire OX11 0RH
Tel: 0235 833009

***Nuclear Industry Radio-active Waste Executive**

Designing a poster:

One of the most important things that can be done is to make more people aware of the dangers of nuclear waste. One way you can do this is to make a poster to hang up at school.

1) Think up a striking and clever heading for the poster which will grab the attention of the viewers.

2) Design an illustration or symbol like the one shown here or cut pictures out of magazines and make a montage that conveys the main theme.

3) Read through this book and try to summarise in about 30 – 40 words why nuclear waste poses a health threat and why it is a problem that will be with us for generations.

4) Again by reading through the book make some suggestions as to how we can solve the problems of nuclear waste management and energy production.

5) Include some other information if there is room, such as useful addresses to contact for more information.

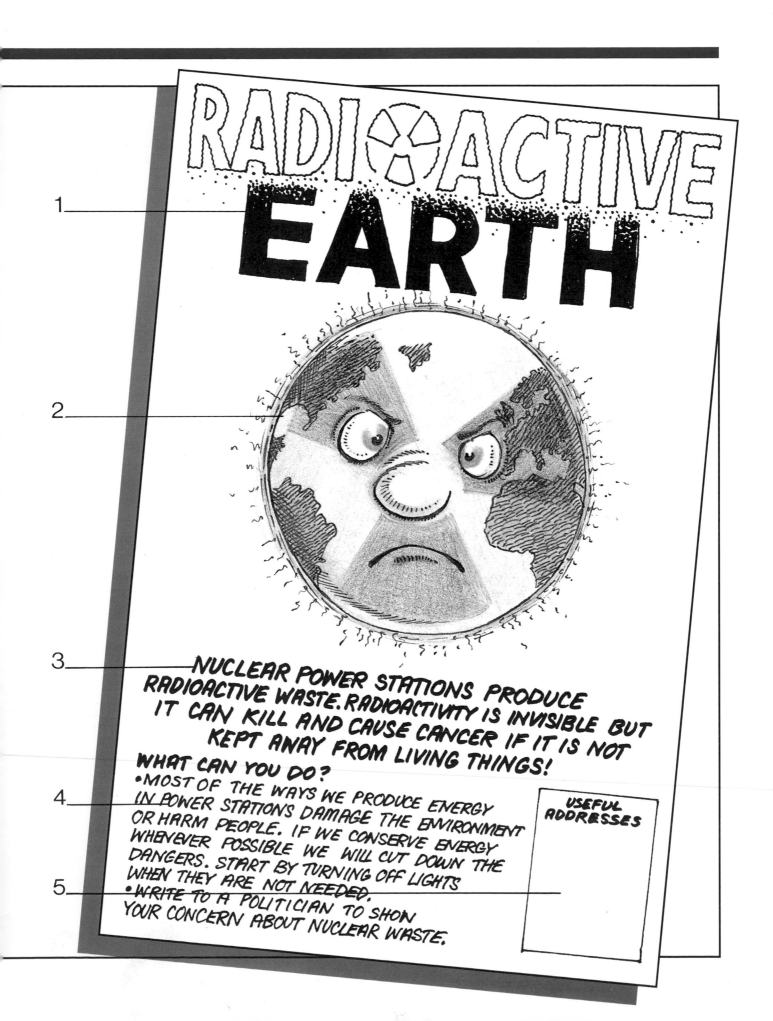

RADIO☢ACTIVE EARTH

1

2

3 NUCLEAR POWER STATIONS PRODUCE RADIOACTIVE WASTE. RADIOACTIVITY IS INVISIBLE BUT IT CAN KILL AND CAUSE CANCER IF IT IS NOT KEPT AWAY FROM LIVING THINGS!

WHAT CAN YOU DO?

4 • MOST OF THE WAYS WE PRODUCE ENERGY IN POWER STATIONS DAMAGE THE ENVIRONMENT OR HARM PEOPLE. IF WE CONSERVE ENERGY WHENEVER POSSIBLE WE WILL CUT DOWN THE DANGERS. START BY TURNING OFF LIGHTS WHEN THEY ARE NOT NEEDED.

5 • WRITE TO A POLITICIAN TO SHOW YOUR CONCERN ABOUT NUCLEAR WASTE.

USEFUL ADDRESSES

FACT FILE 1

Nuclear bombs

In fission, particles split atoms which release more particles and so on, while energy builds up. In nuclear bombs this process is not controlled and the result is the release of a huge amount of energy all at once; a nuclear explosion.

Who uses nuclear power?

France and Belgium get nearly 70 per cent of their energy from nuclear power. The United States gets 20 per cent and the USSR 13 per cent, but both have cancelled many of their planned reactors in the last 15 years because of safety fears.

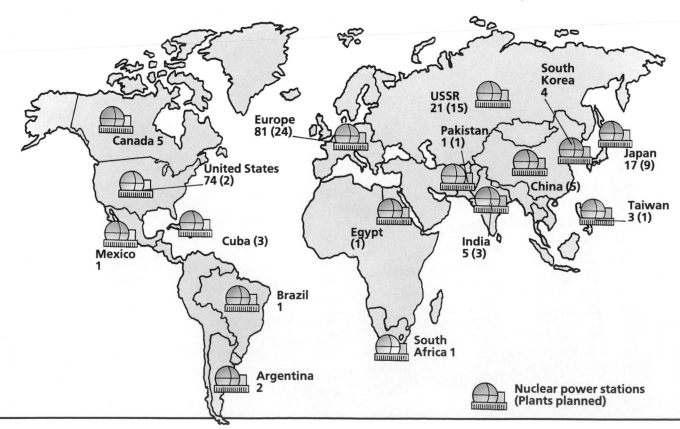

Canada 5

Europe 81 (24)

United States 74 (2)

Cuba (3)

Mexico 1

Brazil 1

Argentina 2

USSR 21 (15)

South Korea 4

Pakistan 1 (1)

Japan 17 (9)

China (5)

Taiwan 3 (1)

Egypt (1)

India 5 (3)

South Africa 1

Nuclear power stations (Plants planned)

Amount of high-level waste

In the United States between 1,000 and 2,000 tonnes of spent fuel are produced every year. This is a tiny amount in comparison to other types of hazardous waste, which equal over 250,000 tonnes a year. The total amount of high-level waste so far generated in the United States would fill an American football stadium to a depth of between eight and 10 metres. However, this nuclear waste is much more difficult to dispose of than other kinds of hazardous waste. And the amount of nuclear waste is growing. In the United States it is estimated that the amount of spent fuel in storage by the end of the century will more than treble.

Amount of high-level waste in the United States: 375,000 cubic metres

10 metres deep

Hidden dangers

Eventually the containers of nuclear waste in deep disposal will corrode. Water could carry the remaining radioactivity into a river. Radioactive gases will be produced. From water or air the radioactivity will enter plants and animals. It has been suggested that harmful doses of radio-activity could be experienced even after millions of years as a result of people consuming contaminated products.

Radioactive gas into air

Radioactive crops

Radioactive fish and drinking water

Radioactive milk from contaminated cows

Leaking waste storage

Radiation in soil and groundwater

FACT FILE 2

Nuclear space craft

Nuclear power is used in space as well as on Earth. Low-flying secret missions often use nuclear power rather than the solar panels used by many space craft, because these panels catch the wind at low altitude and affect the craft's flight. Nuclear power is also used deep in space when the Sun is too far away to supply enough solar energy. The deep-space probe *Galileo*, which began its six-year journey to Jupiter in 1989, contains two nuclear reactors. It is due to investigate the planet for 20 months.

Decommissioning

A nuclear power station, like any structure, begins to deteriorate after a certain amount of time. At this point it has to be decommissioned: closed down and taken apart. Waste Chem (below) is a British company which exists for special projects like decommissioning and radioactive waste management. So far, no large-scale nuclear power stations have been decommissioned, so we do not have much experience of problems that can arise, but experts believe that decommissioning is potentially dangerous. The building materials at nuclear power stations are contaminated with radioactivity and generate a large amount of low-level waste. The reactor itself is highly contaminated. Present plans for decommissioning some nuclear power stations involve leaving the reactor for 100 years and then cutting it up behind glass by remote control. Decommissioning, like nuclear waste, is a problem that we are passing on to future generations.

GLOSSARY

Atoms – tiny particles which make up everything. They consist of even smaller particles called protons, neutrons and electrons.

Control rod – a rod which can absorb some of the neutrons produced during nuclear fission in a nuclear reactor. The rod usually contains substances such as cadmium or boron and is used to prevent fission from running out of control.

Decommissioning – closing down, taking apart and making safe old nuclear power stations.

Fission – the splitting of an atom. This process releases energy and radiation and occurs naturally as well as being used in nuclear power stations and nuclear weapons.

Fusion – joining together of atoms. This releases energy and scientists hope to harness it in the future for use in power stations, although so far this has proved difficult. Fusion is the form of energy production in stars.

Half-life – the length of time taken for a radioactive substance to decay to half of its original amount. Each different radioactive material has a specific half-life.

Moderator – a substance, like graphite or water, used in a nuclear reactor to slow neutrons down to a speed at which they are most effective in causing fission.

Radiation – a way of transferring energy from one place to another, usually by rays.

Radioactivity – comes from the decay of unstable atoms. This process results in the production of tiny particles and sometimes rays. Some types of radioactivity are extremely damaging to living things and can stay dangerous for thousands of years.

Reprocessing – the treatment of spent nuclear fuel rods to extract the remaining uranium, which may be used to make more fuel. Another radioactive metal, plutonium, is also extracted. It can be used in nuclear weapons or to make more fuel.

Spent fuel – used up fuel from a nuclear reactor. It still contains some of the radioactive material which can undergo fission, but not enough to power the nuclear reactor efficiently.

Uranium – a radioactive metal found naturally in some types of rock, for example granite.

INDEX

Photographic Credits:
Cover and pages 11 bottom, 13, 16 and 18: British Nuclear Fuels Limited; pages 4-5, 12, 21 and 23: Topham Picture Library; pages 6 left and 7: Robert Harding Photo Library; pages 6 right and 30 bottom: The Environmental Picture Library; page 9 left: UKAEA; pages 9 right, 14 and 28: Frank Spooner Pictures; page 11 top: J. Allan Cash Photo Library; page 17: Spectrum Photo Library; page 22: Panos Pictures; pages 25 and 30 top: Science Photo Library.